MACMILLAN PRIMARY INTEGRATED READING

Louis Fidge and Sue Graves

**Advisers: Janet McLeish   Kaydeen Miles-McLean
Sonia Mills   Shirla Taffe   Sandra Wiggan**

Contents

Term 1

Unit 1	Hello	4
Unit 2	Lenny and Lizzy can	8
Unit 3	The birthday party	11
Unit 4	Judy-Ann	15
Unit 5	My body is amazing	19
Rhyme time 1		22
Unit 6	This is you!	24
Unit 7	The enormous yam	28
Unit 8	Market day	32
Unit 9	Brother Breeze and the pear tree	35
Unit 10	Chickenpox	39
Rhyme time 2		42

Term 2

Unit 11	Grandpa's big family	44
Unit 12	The busy day	48
Unit 13	Vegetables for dinner	51
Unit 14	The picnic	55
Unit 15	Special days and national symbols	58
Rhyme time 3		62

Unit 16	Lenny and Lizzy and the Big Parade	64
Unit 17	Kevin's new house	68
Unit 18	The kitchen	72
Unit 19	One windy night	75
Unit 20	The hot pan	79
Rhyme time 4		82

Term 3

Unit 21	Our school	84
Unit 22	Playtime is best	88
Unit 23	Dan the dinosaur comes to school	91
Unit 24	Good school – better school!	95
Unit 25	The fire drill	99
Rhyme time 5		102
Unit 26	Silly Sam	104
Unit 27	People at school	108
Unit 28	Lenny and Lizzy at the hospital	112
Unit 29	Sports day	115
Unit 30	The school party	119
Rhyme time 6		122
Word list		124

1 Hello

Hello. My name is Ashley Bell.
My first name is Ashley.
My last name is Bell.
I am a girl.
I am six years old.

Hello.

This is my school.
This is Miss Green.
Miss Green is my teacher.
I like Miss Green.
I like my school.

This is my house.
I live in my house with my mother.
I live in my house with my father, too.
Can you see my mother?
Can you see my father?

1

2 Is Ashley a boy or a girl?
3 How old is Ashley?
4 What is the name of Ashley's teacher?
5

Is this Ashley's house or school?
6 Who lives in the house with Ashley?

1 What is your name?
2 How old are you?
3 Are you a boy or a girl?
4 What is the name of your teacher?
5 What is the name of your school?
6 Who lives in your house with you?

2 Lenny and Lizzy can

'Look! I can jump,' said Lenny.
'Look! I can jump, too,' said Lizzy.
'Look! I can hop,' said Lenny.
'Look! I can hop, too,' said Lizzy.

'Look! I can run,' said Lizzy
'Look! I can run, too,' said Lenny.
'I like to play,' said Lizzy.
'I like to play, too!' said Lenny.

Match each sentence with the correct picture.

a Lenny can jump. **d** Lizzy can jump.
b Lenny can hop.   **e** Lizzy can hop.
c Lenny can run.   **f** Lizzy can run.

1  2  3

4  5  6

1 Talk about some things you can do.
2 Talk about some things you can't do.
3 What sort of games do you like to play:
 a) on your own?
 b) with another person?
 c) with more than one person?

3 The birthday party

It was Mark's birthday.
He was happy.
Mark looked for Grandma.
'Where is Grandma?' he said.

Mark's friends danced.
Mark's friends sang.
Mark looked for Grandma.
'Where is Grandma?' he said.

Then Grandma came.
Mark was happy.
'Happy birthday, Mark,' Grandma said.
Grandma gave Mark a cake.
'Thank you, Grandma,' Mark said.

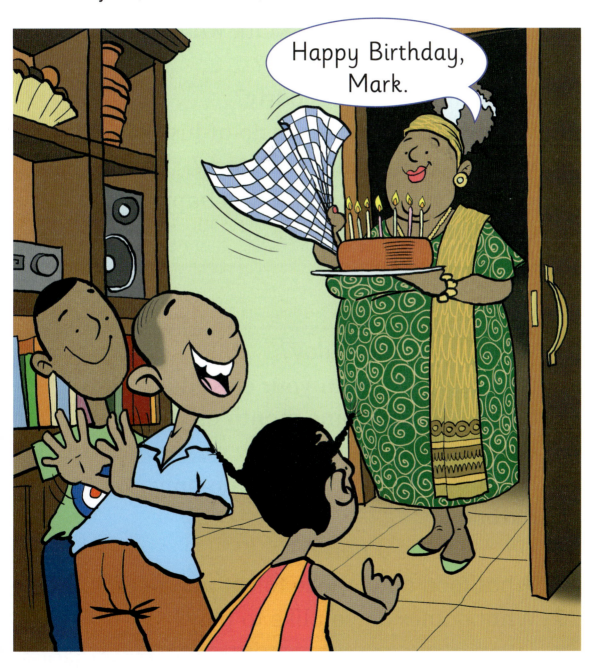

1  What is my name?

2 Whose birthday was it?
3 How old do you think Mark was?
4 Whom did Mark look for?
5 Who came to Mark's party?
6 What did Mark's friends do at his party?
7 What did Grandma give Mark?
8 Why do you think Mark was happy when Grandma came?

1 When is your birthday?
2 Does anyone else in your class have a birthday in the same month as you?
3 Can you find your birthday on a calendar?
4 What sort of things do you do on your birthday?
5 Do you have a party?
6 What food do you like to eat at a party?
7 What games do you like to play?

4 Judy-Ann

Judy-Ann liked her name.
Mummy said, 'My name is Judy. You are called Judy like me. You are special to me.'

Aunt Ann said, 'My name is Ann.
You are called Ann, like me.
You are special to me.'

Grandma said, 'My name is Judy-Ann.
You are called Judy-Ann, like me.
You are special to me.'
'I like my special name,' Judy-Ann said.

1 What is my name?

2   3   4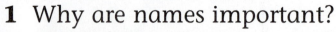

   Who is this?   Who is this?   Who is this?

5 Whose name is Judy?
6 Whose name is Ann?
7 Whose name is Judy-Ann?
8 Does Judy-Ann like her name?

1 Why are names important?
2 Do you know how you got your name?
3 Does your name have a special meaning?
4 Does anyone else in your family have the same name as you?
5 Can you think of a boy or girl's name beginning with each letter of the alphabet? For example:
A – **A**nn   B – **B**en   C – **C**arla
and so on.

5 My body is amazing

My body is amazing.
I have two legs.
My legs can run.

I have two hands.
My hands can pick ackee.

I have two eyes.
My eyes can see.

I have a nose.
My nose can smell.

I have two ears.
My ears can hear.

I have a mouth.
My mouth can eat.
My mouth can talk.

My body is amazing!

Choose the best word to complete each sentence.
1. I can run with my _____ (hands, legs).
2. I can pick ackee with my _____ (hands, legs).
3. I can smell with my _____ (mouth, nose).
4. I can hear with my _____ (nose, ears).
5. I can eat and talk with my _____ (ears, mouth).

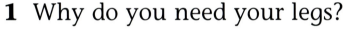

1. Why do you need your legs?
2. List all the things you can do with your hands.
3. What smells do you like? What smells don't you like?
4. Keep quiet for a minute. What sounds can you hear?
5. Why is your mouth important?
6. Name different parts of your body.
7. What letter does each part of your body begin with?

   Example: **l** for **l**eg, **h** for **h**and.

Rhyme time 1

Things I can do

I can count and I can run.
I can climb a tree.
I can skip and I can hop.
I can swim in the sea.
I can clap and I can jump.
I can sing and hum.
I can draw and I can read
I can hug my mum!

Things I like

I like my ball and my bat.
I like my home and my hat.
I like my cat and my coat.
I like my Grandma and her goat.
I like my pencils and my pens.
I like my fish and all my friends.
I *don't* like it when I'm sad.
But I do like playing with my dad!

6 This is you!

Mummy was looking at a book.
Eric looked at the book, too.
'Who is this?' Eric said.
'This is you,' Mummy said. 'You were a baby.
You could not walk. You could not talk.'

'Who is this?' Eric said.
'This is you,' Mummy said. 'You were two years old.
You could walk and you could talk!'
'Who is this?' Eric said.
'This is you,' Mummy said. 'You were four years
old. Look! You could ride a bicycle.'

'I am a big boy now. I am six years old,' Eric said. 'I can walk and I can talk. I can ride a bicycle. Look! I can climb a tree!'

Discuss and write

Say if each sentence is **true** or **false**.
1 Mummy was looking at a book with Eric.
2 When Eric was a baby he could walk.
3 When Eric was a baby he could not talk.
4 When Eric was two he could talk.
5 When Eric was four he had a bicycle.
6 Eric said, 'I am a big boy now.'
7 Eric is seven years old.
8 Eric can climb a tree.

Talkabout

1 Talk about some things a baby can do.
2 Talk about some things a baby can't do.
3 Do you have any younger brothers or sisters? Talk about the things they can and cannot do.
4 How have you changed since you came to school?
5 Do you have any older brothers or sisters? How are they different from you?

7 The enormous yam

The farmer planted a yam.
It grew and grew.
It grew into an enormous yam.
'What an enormous yam!' the farmer said.
'I will pull it out.'
The farmer pulled and pulled the enormous yam.
He could not pull it out.

'I will help you,' the farmer's wife said.
They pulled and pulled the enormous yam.
They could not pull it out.
'I will help you,' Goat said.
They pulled and pulled the enormous yam.
They could not pull it out.

'I will help you,' Dog said.
They pulled and pulled the enormous yam.
Out came the enormous yam.

1. What did the farmer plant?
2. What did it grow into?
3. Could the farmer pull the enormous yam out?
4. Who helped the farmer?
5. Which animal helped the farmer and his wife?
6. Which animal helped the farmer and his wife and the goat?
7. What noise do you think the yam made when they pulled it out?

1. What does a plant need to make it grow?
2. How many different vegetables can you name?
3. What sound does each vegetable begin with?
Example: carrot begins with **c**.
4. What vegetables do you like?
5. Are there any vegetables you don't like?
6. Talk about where we get our vegetables from.
7. Why are farmers important?

8 Market day

It was market day.
'We need some fish,' Aunt Bessy said.
'Fish helps you to grow big and strong.'
'I like to grow big and strong,' Annie said.

'We need some pumpkin,' Aunt Bessy said.
'Pumpkin helps you to run and jump.'
'I like to run and jump,' said Annie.
Leon gave Annie a mango. 'This mango is for you,'
Leon said. 'Mango helps to keep you fit and well.'
'Thank you, Leon,' said Annie. 'I like to keep fit
and well.'

Complete the sentences.
1 _____ and _____ went to the market.
2 Fish helps you to grow _____ and _____ .
3 After the fish, Aunt Bessy got some _____ .
4 Pumpkin helps you to _____ and _____ .
5 Leon gave _____ a _____ .
6 Mango helps to keep you _____ and _____ .
7 At the market Aunt Bessy and Annie got some _____ , _____ and _____ .

1 Why do we need food?
2 Where do we get fish from?
3 Do you eat pumpkin at home?
4 Do you know how mangoes grow?
5 Would you like to work in a market?
6 What sort of food is good for us?

9 Brother Breeze and the pear tree

Anancy had a pear tree.
Brother Breeze blew the pears off the tree!
Anancy was upset.
He went to see Brother Breeze.
Brother Breeze gave Anancy a cloth.
'Say, "*Spread, cloth, spread!*" and the cloth will give you some food,' said Brother Breeze.

Anancy said, '*Spread, cloth, spread!*' The cloth gave Anancy some food.
Anancy was greedy. He wanted lots of food.
One day the cloth did not work!

Anancy was upset.
He went to see Brother Breeze.
'The cloth will not work!' he said.
Brother Breeze gave Anancy a stick.
'Say, "*Beat, stick, beat!*" to the stick,'
said Brother Breeze.
Anancy said, '*Beat, stick, beat!*'
The stick beat Anancy!
'That will teach you!' said Brother
Breeze. 'Do not be greedy!'

Choose the correct answers.

1. What did Anancy have?
   a) an apple tree   b) a pear tree
2. Who blew the pears off the tree?
   a) Anancy   b) Brother Breeze
3. What did Brother Breeze give to Anancy first?
   a) a cloth   b) a stick
4. What did the cloth give Anancy?
   a) some food   b) some books
5. What happened when Anancy was greedy?
   a) The cloth stopped working.
   b) The cloth gave him lots of food.
6. What did Brother Breeze give Anancy next?
   a) some pears   b) a stick
7. What happened when Anancy said, '*Beat, stick, beat!*'?
   a) The stick stopped working.
   b) The stick beat Anancy.

1. Do you think Anancy was greedy?
2. Why is it wrong to be greedy?
3. Talk about the sorts of food you like to eat.

10 Chickenpox

Ben was sad.
He felt hot.
Mummy looked at Ben.
Ben had spots.
'You have chickenpox,' Mummy said. 'Go to bed.'
'I don't want to go to bed,' Ben said. 'I want to play.'

Ben was very sad.
He felt very hot.
Mummy put some medicine on the spots.
The medicine felt cool.
Ben felt cool.
'Can I play now?' he said.
'No,' Mummy said. 'Wait for the spots to go.
Then you can play.'

Discuss and write

Choose the best word for each sentence.
1 Ben was _____ (happy, sad).
2 Ben felt _____ (hot, cold).
3 Ben had _____ (pots, spots).
4 Ben's Mummy said, 'Go to _____ (school, bed).'
5 Ben's Mummy put some _____ (medicine, milk) on the spots.
6 The medicine felt _____ (cool, cold).
7 Ben wanted to go out to _____ (pay, play).
8 Ben's Mummy said, 'Wait for the spots to _____ (come, go).'

Talkabout

1 Have you ever been ill? Talk about what happened.
2 How can a doctor help us?
3 How does medicine help us?
4 Why must you never touch medicine unless a grown-up is with you?

Rhyme time 2

To market, to market

To market, to market
To buy some rice.
Home again, home again.
Very nice!

To market, to market
To buy some peas.
Home again, home again,
If you please!

To market, to market
To buy some meat.
Home again, home again.
Time to eat!

Miss Polly

Miss Polly had a dolly who was sick, sick, sick.
She called for the doctor to come quick, quick, quick.
The doctor came with his bag and his hat.
He knocked on the door with a rat-a-tat-tat.
He looked at the dolly and he shook his head.
He said, 'Miss Polly put her straight to bed.'
He wrote on some paper for a pill, pill, pill.
'That will make it better, yes, it will, will, will.'

11 Grandpa's big family

It is Grandpa's birthday.
A man is taking pictures of the family.
The man is taking a picture of Grandpa.
Grandpa is the oldest in the family.
The man is taking some pictures of Aunt Jess and Uncle Tom.
Aunt Jess is Grandpa's daughter.
Uncle Tom is Grandpa's son.
Grandpa is their father.

The man is taking some pictures of Rosie, Lamar and Ben.
They are Grandpa's grandchildren.
Grandpa is their grandfather.
The man is taking a picture of baby Lavan.
Baby Lavan is Grandpa's great-grandson.
Baby Lavan is the youngest in the family.
Grandpa is his great-grandfather.

Grandpa puts his picture on the wall.
Next he puts the pictures of Aunt Jess and Uncle Tom on the wall.
Next he puts the pictures of Rosie, Lamar and Ben on the wall.
Last of all, he puts the picture of baby Lavan on the wall.
What a big family!

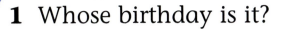

1. Whose birthday is it?
2. Why do you think the man is taking pictures of the family?
3. Is Grandpa the oldest or youngest in the family?
4. Who is Grandpa's daughter?
5. Who is Grandpa's son?
6. Who are Grandpa's grandchildren?
7. Who is Grandpa's great-grandson?
8. Is Baby Lavan the oldest or youngest in the family?
9. Where does Grandpa put the pictures?

1. Who is the oldest and youngest in your family?
2. How many of your uncles and aunts can you name?
3. Tell the class something interesting about one person in your family.
4. Do you have any brothers or sisters?
5. Where do you come in your family (for example, are you the oldest child)?

12 The busy day

Mummy was very busy in the kitchen.
'I am very busy,' Mummy said.
'I can help you,' Lester said.
Lester swept the floor.
He put the food in the fridge.
He washed the dishes.
Then the baby began to cry.

'Oh no!' Mummy said. 'I am very busy.'
'I can help you,' Clement said.
Clement fed the baby.
Clement played with the baby.
'Thank you for your help, Lester. Thank you for your help, Clement,' Mummy said.
'I like to help,' Lester said.
'I like to help, too!' Clement said.

Mummy **Lester** **Clement**

Who…
1 … was very busy?
2 … swept the floor?
3 … fed the baby?
4 … put the food in the fridge?
5 … played with the baby?
6 … washed the dishes?
7 … said 'Thank you'?

1 List some of the things your Mummy does in your house.
2 Do you think it is important to help at home?
3 What sort of things can you do to help?
4 Why is it important to say 'Please' and 'Thank you'?

13 Vegetables for dinner

Every day, Grandpa worked in his garden.
He grew lots of vegetables.
Every day, Grandpa picked some vegetables for dinner.
It was hard work.
Every day, Grandma cooked the dinner.
She cut up the vegetables.
Every day, Grandma cooked the vegetables in a big pot.
It was hard work.

One day Grandpa fell over.
He fell over and hurt his arm.
Grandpa said, 'Oh no! I can't pick the vegetables for dinner.'
Grandma said, 'Oh no! I have no vegetables. I can't cook the dinner!'
'I will pick the vegetables for you,' Paul said.

Paul went into the garden.
He picked lots of vegetables.
It was hard work!
Grandma cut up the vegetables.
She cooked the dinner.
She cooked the vegetables in a big pot.
Grandma was happy. Grandpa was happy, too.
'Thank you for picking the vegetables, Paul,'
they said.

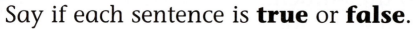

Say if each sentence is **true** or **false**.
1 Every day, Grandma worked in the garden.
2 Grandpa grew lots of vegetables.
3 Every day, Grandpa picked some vegetables for dinner.
4 Every day, Grandpa cooked the dinner.
5 Grandma cut up the vegetables.
6 Grandma cooked the vegetables in a small pot.
7 One day Grandpa fell over and hurt his leg.
8 Paul picked the vegetables for Grandpa.
9 It was hard work.

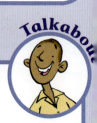

1 Why do you think Grandpa grew vegetables in his garden?
2 Why do you think it was hard work?
3 Why do we need food?
4 Do you think Grandma worked as hard as Grandpa?
5 Do you think Paul is a kind boy?

14 The picnic

Miss Brown: It is Children's Day tomorrow. Let's have a picnic.
Everyone: Yes, let's have a picnic!
Miss Brown: Let's bring some food to share.
May-Ling: I am from China. I will bring some vegetables and noodles.
Gopal: I am from India. I will bring some curry and rice.
Dexter: I am from Jamaica. I will bring some ackee and saltfish.

Miss Brown: Do you like the food, children?
Dexter: Yes, I like the curry and rice.
May-Ling: Yes, I like the ackee and saltfish.
Gopal: Yes, I like the vegetables and noodles.
Miss Brown: Do you like the picnic, children?
Everyone: Yes, the picnic is fun.

Miss Brown   **Dexter**   **May-Ling**   **Gopal**

Who said …

1 It is Children's Day tomorrow.
2 Let's bring some food to share.
3 I am from India. I will bring some curry and rice.
4 I am from Jamaica. I will bring some ackee and saltfish.
5 I am from China. I will bring some vegetables and noodles.
6 Do you like the food, children?
7 I like the curry and rice.
8 I like the ackee and saltfish.
9 I like the vegetables and noodles.
10 The picnic is fun.

1 Do you like picnics?
2 Do you ever go for a picnic with your family?
3 Do you like to try different sorts of food?

15 Special days and national symbols

Special days

In Jamaica we have lots of special days.

May 23rd is Labour Day.
Last Labour Day, we worked hard at our school.
We cleaned the yard.
We cleaned all the windows.
Our parents worked hard at our school, too.

Independence Day is an important day.
It is on August 6th.
But there are lots of celebrations before August 6th!
There are Speech Festivals. There are Drama Festivals. There are Song Festivals and a Festival Queen Contest, too.
On Independence Day the winners and runners-up join in a Big Parade.
Everyone likes to watch the Big Parade on Independence Day.

National symbols

In Jamaica we have lots of national symbols.

National flag

"This is our national flag."

Blue mahoe tree

"The blue mahoe is our national tree."

Ackee

"The ackee is our national fruit."

Lignum vitae

"The lignum vitae is our national flower."

The Doctor Bird

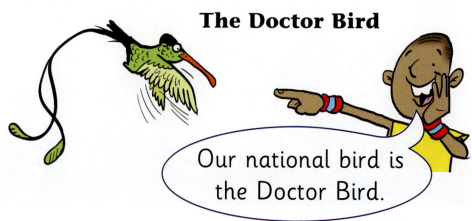

"Our national bird is the Doctor Bird."

Discuss and write

1 Why is May 23rd a special day?
2 What did the children and their parents do last Labour Day?
3 What do children do every year on August 6th?
4 What is this?

5 What is the name of Jamaica's:
   a) national fruit?   b) national flower?
   c) national tree?   d) national bird?

Talkabout

1 What special days do you celebrate:
   a) with your family?
   b) at school?
2 What sort of thing do you do on these special days?
3 Which special day do you like best?

Rhyme time 3

Thank you for the world so sweet

Thank you for the world so sweet.
Thank you for the food we eat.
Thank you for the birds that sing.
Thank you, God, for everything.

A baby

A baby likes to creep.
A baby likes to hide.
A baby likes to sleep.
A baby likes to slide.
A baby likes to shout.
A baby likes to throw.
A baby likes to eat.
A baby likes to grow.

16 Lenny and Lizzy and the Big Parade

It was Independence Day.
Lenny and Lizzy were excited.
'It is the Big Parade this afternoon,' Mummy said.
'Hurray!' Lenny said.
'Let's dress up for the Big Parade,' Lizzy said.

Mummy opened a box.
In the box there was a big bag.
In the big bag there were lots of feathers.
There were some green feathers in the big bag.
There were some red feathers in the big bag.
There were some yellow feathers in the big bag, too.
'Let's dress up as Doctor Birds!' Lizzy said.
'Yes. Let's dress up as Doctor Birds!' Lenny said.

Let's dress up as Doctor Birds!

There were lots of clowns at the Big Parade.
There was a band, too.
Everyone cheered the clowns. Everyone cheered the band.
'Hurray for the clowns! Hurray for the band!' they said.
Then everyone saw the two Doctor Birds.
Everyone cheered the Doctor Birds.
'Hurray for the Doctor Birds!' they said. 'Hurray for Lizzy and Lenny!'

Choose the correct answers.
1. It was
   a) Emancipation Day   **b)** Independence Day.
2. There was a   **a)** Big Parade   **b)** Big Picnic.
3. Mummy opened a   **a)** box   **b)** book.
4. In the box there was a
   a) big bag   **b)** big boy.
5. In the bag there were some
   a) vegetables   **b)** feathers.
6. The children dressed up as
   a) Doctor Birds   **b)** trees.
7. At the Big Parade there was a
   a) band   **b)** hand.

1. How do you celebrate Independence Day?
2. Have you ever dressed up?
3. Have you ever seen a Big Parade?
4. What sort of places do you go to with your family?
5. What sort of things do you do together with your family?

17 Kevin's new house

Kevin was excited.
He was moving to a new house.
He was moving to a new house with his mummy and daddy.
They went to their new house in a big truck.
Lots of people said, 'Hello. Welcome to your new house.'

'We will help you,' the people said.
'Can I help, too?' said Kevin.
His daddy said, 'Yes, you can.'
First, Kevin saw a bed.
'The bed goes in the bedroom,' he said.
Next, Kevin saw a stove.
'The stove goes in the kitchen,' he said.

Then, Kevin saw a sofa,
'The sofa goes in the living room,' he said.
Last of all, Kevin saw a box.
'What is in this box?' he said.
'This box is for you,' the people said. 'Welcome to your new house.'

Match up each sentence beginning with the correct sentence ending.

1 Kevin went to his new house in
2 Lots of people said,
3 The bed went in
4 The stove went in
5 The sofa went in
6 The people gave Kevin

a a box.
b the living room.
c a big truck.
d the kitchen.
e the bedroom.
f 'Welcome to your new house.'

1 Do you think Kevin will find it strange, living in a new house?
2 Do you think Kevin will soon make some new friends?
3 Discuss what furniture you have in each room in your house.
4 What is each thing used for?

18 The kitchen

This is the kitchen.
We keep food in the kitchen.
We cook food in the kitchen, too.

This is the fridge.
We keep food in the fridge.
The fridge makes the food cool.

This is a big pot.
Mummy cooks soup in the big pot.

This is the stove.
We cook food on the stove.
The stove makes the food hot.

This is the table.
We sit at the table.
We eat food at the table.

This is the sink.
We wash the pots and pans in the sink.

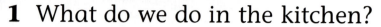

1. What do we do in the kitchen?
2. What do we keep in a fridge?
3. Why do we keep food in a fridge?
4. What does Mummy cook in the big pot?
5. Why do we cook food on a stove?
6. What do we do at the table in the kitchen?
7. What do we wash in the kitchen sink?

1. Name some of the food you keep in a fridge.
2. What are pots and pans made of?
3. Talk about different ways of cooking food.

For example: You can **fry** an egg.

4. Name some things you use when you eat and drink.
5. Do you help in the kitchen at home?

19 One windy night

One night it was very windy.
The wind blew over Aunt May's plant pots.
The wind blew and blew.
It blew down Aunt May's tree.
The wind blew and blew and blew.
It blew off Aunt May's roof.
'Oh no!' said Aunt May. 'Now I have no roof!'

Next day, lots of people came.
The people came to help Aunt May.
'We will build a new roof for you,' they said.
Lewis was a carpenter. He was a good carpenter.
He built a wooden frame for the roof. Lots of people helped.

Sam was a tiler. He was a good tiler. He put new tiles on the roof. Lots of people helped.
Kayleigh was a cleaner. She was a good cleaner. She cleaned up the broken pots. Lots of people helped.
Aunt May was a cook. She was a good cook. She cooked some food for everyone.
'Thank you for my new roof,' she said.

1 Number these sentences in the correct order:

___ The wind blew down Aunt May's tree.
___ The wind blew off Aunt May's roof.
_1_ The wind blew over Aunt May's plant pots.

2 Now number these sentences in the correct order:

___ Sam put new tiles on the roof.
___ Lewis built a wooden frame for the roof.
___ Aunt May cooked some food for all the people.
___ Kayleigh cleaned up the broken pots.

1 Talk about the jobs the following people do:
   a) carpenter   b) plumber
   c) electrician   d) painter
   e) cleaner
2 What do they use to help them do their jobs?
3 What job do you want to do when you grow up?

20 The hot pan

Daddy was cooking the dinner.
Daddy said, 'I am going to the yard. I am going to get some yams from the yard. Don't go near the hot pan, Carmen.'
Daddy went into the yard to get the yams.
Carmen looked at the pan.
She picked up the lid of the pan.
The lid was hot.
Carmen dropped the lid.

Carmen began to cry. Daddy ran in from the yard. 'You silly girl!' Daddy said. 'Never go near a hot pan!'

Carmen was sad. 'I'm sorry,' Carmen said.

Discuss and write

1 Who was cooking the dinner? Daddy or Carmen?
2 Who went into the yard?   Daddy or Carmen?
3 Who said, 'Don't go near the hot pan'? Daddy or Carmen?
4 Who picked up the hot lid of the pan? Daddy or Carmen?
5 Who dropped the hot lid?   Daddy or Carmen?
6 Who began to cry?   Daddy or Carmen?
7 Who ran in from the yard?   Daddy or Carmen?
8 Who said, 'Never go near a hot pan'? Daddy or Carmen?
9 Who was sad?   Daddy or Carmen?
10 Who was a silly girl?   Daddy or Carmen?

Talkabout

1 Why do you think Carmen was a silly girl?
2 What things are dangerous in the kitchen?
3 What things are dangerous in other rooms in your house?
4 Make up some safety rules for your house.

Rhyme time 4

The Big Parade

Stamp your feet
And bang the drum.
The Big Parade
Is lots of fun.

Clowns and bands
And marchers, too,
Let's go and see them,
Me and you.

Let's cheer and shout
Hurray! Hurray!
The Big Parade
Is here today.

In my house

In my house I can hear …
- my daddy singing
- a telephone ringing
- pots and pans clanging
- a door banging
- the wind howling
- a dog growling.

In my house I can smell …
- the coffee my sister is making
- a cake my mummy is baking
- the sweet smell of a flower
- soapy bubbles in the shower
- the shampoo I rub on my head
- some smelly socks under my bed.

21 Our school

This is our school.
This is the car park.
Teachers park their
cars in the car park.

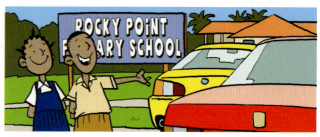

This is the
principal's office.
The principal is in
her office.

This is Grade One.
We work hard in
Grade One.

This is the library.
We read books in
the library.

This is the bathroom.
We wash our hands
in the bathroom.

This is the canteen.
We eat our lunch in the canteen.

This is the staffroom.
Teachers sit in the staffroom.

This is the playground.
We play in the playground.

This is the playing field.
We play games on the playing field.

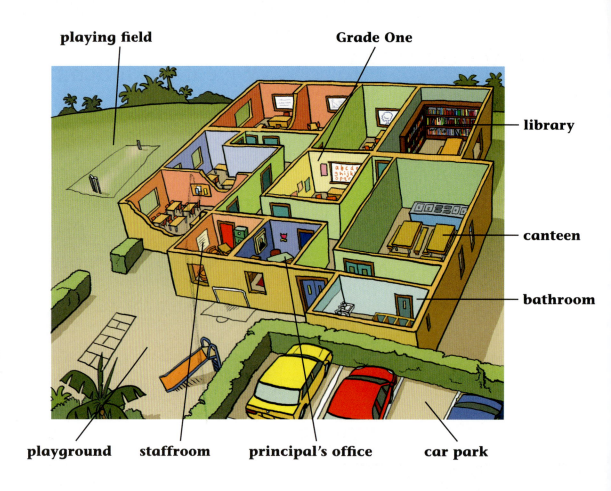

Can you find these places on the plan of our school?

- the car park
- Grade One
- the principal's office
- the staffroom
- the playing field
- the bathroom
- the canteen
- the playground
- the library

Choose the correct answers:
1 The teachers put their cars in the _____ (car park, playground).
2 We wash our hands in the _____ (canteen, bathroom).
3 We eat our lunch in the _____ (library, canteen).
4 We read books in the _____ (library, bathroom).
5 _____ sit in the staffroom. (Teachers, Children)
6 We play in the _____ (principal's office, playground).

1 What is the name and address of your school?
2 What is the name of:
   a) your teacher   b) your principal?
3 Who else works in your school?
4 How many classrooms are there?
5 In what ways is your school the same as Rocky Point Primary School?
6 In what ways is your school different from Rocky Point Primary School?

22 Playtime is best

It was playtime.
Sam and Sandy were in the playground.
'What do you like best at school?' Sam said.
Sandy said, 'I like reading and writing. I like Language Arts best.'
Sam said, 'I like singing and dancing. I like music best.'

Mr Wilson rang the bell.
It was the end of playtime.
Sandy was sad. 'I like playtime,' she said.
Sam was sad. 'I like playtime, too,' he said.
Sandy said, 'I like Language Arts. You like music. We both like playtime. Playtime is best!'

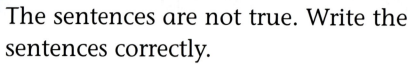

The sentences are not true. Write the sentences correctly.
1 It was time to go home.
2 Sam and Sandy were in the washroom.
3 'What don't you like at school?' Sam said.
4 Sandy said, 'I like music. I like singing. I like music best.'
5 Sam said, 'I like reading. I like Language Arts best.'
6 Mrs Wilson rang the bell.
7 It was the start of playtime.
8 Sam was happy. 'I like playtime,' he said.
9 Sandy was sad. 'I don't like playtime,' she said.

1 What lessons do you like best at school?
2 Are there any lessons you don't like?
3 What do you like to do at playtime?
4 Is your playground a safe place?

23 Dan the dinosaur comes to school

One day Dan the dinosaur came to school.
Dan was very big.
He broke the door.
Dan was very heavy.
He broke his chair.
He broke his desk, too!
His tail was very long.
It broke the window.

Dan wrote in his book.
He broke his pencil.
Dan painted a picture.
He broke his paintbrush.

At the end of the day, Dan went home.

Next day Dan did not come to school.
We worked very hard!

Number these sentences in order.

___ Dan broke the door.
_1_ Dan the Dinosaur came to school.
___ Dan broke his chair.
___ Dan broke his pencil.
___ Dan broke his desk.
___ Dan went home.
___ Dan broke the window.
___ Dan broke his paintbrush.

1. Do you think Dan was a friendly or fierce dinosaur?
2. How would you feel if Dan came to your school?
3. Talk about the damage Dan might do at your school.
4. Talk about some of the fun you could have with Dan at school.
5. Who looks after your school and keeps it clean?

24 Good school – better school!

Jasmine: Our school is a good school, but can we make it better?
Mary: There is garbage in the yard.
Kevin: It's bad to have garbage in the yard.
Jasmine: What can we do?
Mary: We can pick up the garbage. We can put it in the bins.
Jasmine: That will make our school better!

Jasmine: Our school is a good school, but can we make it better?
Mary: There are weeds on the path.
Kevin: It's bad to have weeds on the path.
Jasmine: What can we do?
Mary: We can pull up the weeds. We can put them in the bins.
Jasmine: That will make our school better!

Jasmine: Our school is a good school, but can we make it better?
Mary: There is mud on the floor.
Kevin: It's bad to have mud on the floor.
Jasmine: What can we do?
Mary: We can mop up the mud.
Everyone: Our school was good but now it is better!

Discuss and

1. What are the names of the children in the story?
2. Who wanted to make the school a better place?
3. Who said, 'It's bad to have garbage in the yard'?
4. What did Mary say they should do with the garbage?
5. Who said, 'There are weeds on the path'?
6. What did Mary say they should do with the weeds?
7. What was there on the floor?
8. What did Mary say they should do about the mud?
9. Who said, 'Our school was good, but now it is better!'

Talkabout

1. Why do you think the children wanted to make their school a better place?
2. Why do you think it is bad to have garbage in the yard at school?
3. Can you think of any ways to make your school a better place?

25 The fire drill

One day Mr Jackson went to school.
Mr Jackson was a fireman.
Mr Jackson went to Grade One.
Mr Jackson talked to the children in Grade One.
Mr Jackson talked to the children about fire.
'When the fire bell rings, go into the yard.
Walk. Do not run,' he said.

Brrring! Brrring! The fire bell rang.
The children went into the yard.
They walked.
They did not run.
'Well done, children,' Mr Jackson said.
'I can't see a fire,' Andrew said.
'There is no fire,' Mr Jackson said. 'It was just a fire drill!'

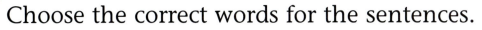

Choose the correct words for the sentences.
1. Mr Jackson was a _____ (policeman, fireman).
2. He talked to the children in Grade _____ (One, Two).
3. He talked to the children about _____ (garbage, fire).
4. He told the children to go into the _____ (yard, classroom) when the fire bell rang.
5. The fire bell went _____ (Pop! Brrring!)
6. The children _____ (walked, ran) into the yard.
7. Andrew said, 'I can't see a _____ (weed, fire).'
8. Mr Jackson said, 'It was just a fire _____ (drill, drum).'

1. What would you do if there was a fire in your school?
2. Why do you think Mr Jackson told the children to walk, not run, into the yard?
3. Which places in your school are safe for you?
4. Which places in your school are unsafe for you? Why?

Rhyme time 5

A day at school

In the classroom

Paint a picture.
Read a book.
Listen to a story.
Count and cook.

In the playground

Hop and skip.
Run and jump.
Throw a ball.
Bump! Bump! Bump!

In the canteen

Time to eat.
Yum, yum, yum!
Lots of food
In my tum, tum, tum!

Sounds in school

Doors slamming,
Children singing,
Clocks ticking,
Bells ringing.
Children laughing,
Music playing,
Teachers talking
Children praying.
Balls bouncing,
Hands clapping,
Feet running,
Feet tapping.

26 Silly Sam

One day, Mr Nelson said, 'Look at this. Do not run in school!'
But Sam did not listen.

The bell rang.
Sam ran out of the door.
He bumped into Annie. Annie fell over. She was upset.
'Silly Sam!' Annie said. 'Do not run in school!'
But Sam did not listen.
Then Sam bumped into Ben. Ben fell over. He was very upset.
'Silly Sam!' Ben said. 'Do not run in school!'
But Sam did not listen.

Sam ran down the stairs.
Sam ran very fast.
He bumped into Miss Williams!
Sam fell over.
Miss Williams fell over.
Miss Williams was very, very upset!
'Silly Sam!' she said. 'Do not run in school!'
Sam was sad.
'I'm sorry!' he said.

1 What did Mr Nelson tell the children?
2 Who did not listen?
3 What did Sam do when the bell rang?
4 Whom did Sam bump into first?
5 What did Annie do?
6 How did Annie feel?
7 Whom did Sam bump into next?
8 **a)** What did Ben do? **b)** How did Ben feel?
9 Whom did Sam bump into on the stairs?
10 Was Sam sorry or glad?

1 Why isn't it safe to run in school?
2 Where is it safe to run at school?
3 Do you have any school rules?
   What are they?
   Why are they important?
5 Think of five sensible rules for your classroom.

27 People at school

This is Mr Winston.
Mr Winston is the principal.
Mr Winston works hard.
He is a good principal.

This is Miss Jones.
Miss Jones is the vice-principal. Miss Jones works hard. She is a good vice-principal.

This is Mr Nelson.
Mr Nelson is a teacher.
Mr Nelson works hard.
He is a good teacher.

This is Miss Smith.
Miss Smith is the school
secretary. Miss Smith
works hard. She is a
good secretary.

This is Mrs Taylor.
Mrs Taylor is the cook.
Mrs Taylor works hard.
She is a good cook.

This is Mr Harris.
Mr Harris is the
watchman. Mr Harris
works hard. He is a good
watchman.

This is Mrs Bell and this is Mrs Porter. Mrs Bell and Mrs Porter are cleaners. Mrs Bell and Mrs Porter work hard. They are good cleaners.

This is Mr Luke. Mr Luke is the janitor. Mr Luke works hard. He is a good janitor.

These are the children. There are lots of children in the school. The children work hard. They are good children.

Name the people. Say what they do.

Discuss and write

Talkabout

1. Name some of the people who work at your school.
2. What job does each person do?
3. Talk to some of the people and find out more about their jobs.
4. Why is each person important?
5. Which person has worked at your school for the longest time?

28 Lenny and Lizzy at the hospital

Andrew fell off his bicycle. He hurt his leg.
He went to the hospital.
Lenny and Lizzy were sad.
'Can we go and see Andrew in hospital?' Lenny said.
'Yes, we can,' Mummy said.
Mummy went to the hospital with Lenny and Lizzy.
Andrew was in bed. Andrew looked sad.
Lenny and Lizzy gave Andrew a big book.
Andrew liked the book. Andrew was happy. 'Thank you,' Andrew said.

A nurse came to see Andrew.
The nurse was wearing a uniform.
'Why are you wearing a uniform?' Lizzy said.
'My uniform tells you I am a nurse,' the nurse said.
'I like your uniform,' said Lizzy. 'One day I want to be a nurse. Then I can wear a uniform like you!'
'A nurse works very hard,' the nurse said. 'But I like my work.'

Andrew   Lenny   Lizzy   Mummy   the nurse

Who …

1 … fell off his bicycle?
2 … hurt his leg?
3 … went to the hospital?
4 … went to the hospital with Lenny and Lizzy?
5 … was in bed?
6 … gave Andrew a book?
7 … was wearing a uniform?
8 … said, 'One day I want to be a nurse'?
9 … said, 'A nurse works very hard'?

1 Describe your school uniform.
2 Why do you wear a uniform at school?
3 Talk about why nurses wear a uniform.
4 Think of as many different people as you can who wear uniforms.
5 Describe their uniforms and talk about why each group of people wear uniforms.

29 Sports Day

Today it is Sports Day.
It is a hot day.
Everyone is excited.
Everyone likes Sports Day.
Sports Day is fun!

Look at Jade. Jade is jumping. She jumps a long way.

Look at Lamar. Lamar is running.

He runs fast. He wins the race.

Look at Jasmine. Jasmine is throwing a ball.

She throws the ball into the net.

Look at Kevin. Kevin is running and jumping.

Kevin runs fast.

He jumps a long way.

It is the end of Sports Day.
Everyone is very excited.
Red House is the winner!
Everyone claps and cheers.
The children in Red House win a big cup.
It is time to go home.
The children are very tired.
Sports Day is fun!

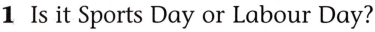
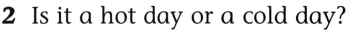

1. Is it Sports Day or Labour Day?
2. Is it a hot day or a cold day?
3. Is everyone sad or excited?
4. Is Jade jumping or running?
5. Does Lamar run fast or slowly?
6. Is Jasmine throwing or kicking a ball?
7. Does Kevin jump a long way or a short way?
8. Is Red House or Blue House the winner?
9. Do Red House win a cup or a mug?

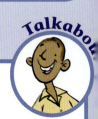

1. What events did the children do at Sports Day in the story?
2. Do you have a Sports Day at school?
   When does it take place?
   Does all the school take part?
   Do your parents come to it?
   What events do you have in it?
3. Do you think Sports Day is fun? Why?

30 The school party

It was the last day of school.
Everyone was excited.
'Let's have a party!' Miss Sharpe said.
Mary swept the floor.
Bevon blew up the balloons.
Cassey put the food on the table.

Let's have a party.

The party was fun.
The children liked the food.
They ate lots of food.
The children played lots of games.
The children liked the games.
They got hot.
Bevon got very hot!
Then Miss Sharpe gave everyone an ice cream.
'You are hot but ice cream is cool,' she said.
The children liked the ice cream.
'Thank you, Miss Sharpe,' the children said.

Discuss and write

Choose the best word for each sentence.
1. It was the _____ (first, last) day of school.
2. Miss Sharpe said, 'Let's have a _____ (race, party).'
3. Mary swept the _____ (door, floor).
4. Bevon blew up the _____ (balls, balloons).
5. The children ate lots of _____ (drinks, food).
6. The children played lots of _____ (games, songs).
7. The children got _____ (cold, hot).
8. Miss Sharpe gave everyone an ice _____ (lolly, cream).

Talkabout

1. Have you ever had a party at school? Talk about when and why you had one.
2. Imagine you are planning a class party.
   - Make two lists – one for food you would like, one for drinks.
   - Where would you get the food and drink?
   - What decorations would you have?
   - What games would you play?

Rhyme time 6

Welcome!

Welcome to the Brownies.
Welcome everyone.
Welcome to the Brownies.
It's time to have some fun!

Welcome to the Cub Scouts.
Welcome everyone.
Welcome to the Cub Scouts.
There's fun for everyone!

The school party

Come to our party!
You can have some fun.
There is a lot to eat
For everyone.

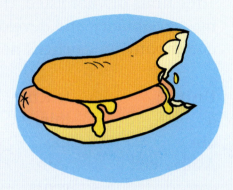

You can eat jello in a bowl,
Green, yellow or pink,
You can eat cookies and cakes
And have juice to drink.

You can eat some sandwiches
With ham and cheese.
But always remember to say
'Thank you' and 'Please'.

You can eat biscuits and sweets,
And cakes and custard,
You can eat pizzas and potato chips
And hot dogs with mustard.

You can eat apple pie
With ice cream on top.
You can eat as much as
you like
Until you go POP!

Word list

Note for teachers:
In Unit 1 each word in the 'Read Together' section is listed. In subsequent units all new words are listed. Words from the Rhyme Time units are not listed. (For suggestions on how to introduce new vocabulary and develop word recognition skills please see the accompanying teacher's notes in the Teacher's Book.)

Unit 1
a
am
Ashley Bell
can
father
first
girl
hello
house
I
in
is
last
like
live
Miss Green
mother
my
name
old
school
see
six
teacher
this
too
with
years
you

Unit 2
hop
jump
Lenny
Lizzy
look
play
run
said
to

Unit 3
birthday
cake
came
danced
for
friends
gave
Grandma
happy
he
it
looked
Mark
Mark's
sang
thank you
then
was
where

Unit 4
Ann
Aunt Ann
are
called
her
Judy
Judy-Ann
like
liked
me
Mummy
special

Unit 5
ackee
amazing
body
ears
eat
eyes
hands
have
hear
legs
mouth
nose
pick
smell
talk
two

Unit 6
and
at
baby
bicycle
big
book
boy
climb
could
Eric
four
looking
not
now
ride
the
tree
walk
were
who

Unit 7
an
Dog
enormous
farmer
farmer's
Goat
grew
help
into
out
planted
pop!

pull
pulled
they
what
wife
will
yam

Unit 8
Annie
Aunt Bessy
day
fish
fit
grow
helps
Leon
keep
mango
market
need
pumpkin
some
strong
we
well

Unit 9
Anancy
be
beat
blew
Brother Breeze
cloth
did

do
food
give
greedy
had
lots
of
off
one
ow!
pear
pears
say
spread
stick
teach
that
upset
wanted
went
work

Unit 10
bed
Ben
chickenpox
cool
don't
felt
go
hot
medicine
no
on
put

sad
spots
very
wait
want

Unit 11
all
Aunt Jess
daughter
family
grandchildren
grandfather
Grandpa
Grandpa's
great-grandfather
great-grandson
his
Lamar
Lavan
man
next
oldest
picture
pictures
puts
Rosie
son
taking
their
Uncle Tom
wall
youngest

125

Unit 12
began
busy
Clement
cry
dishes
fed
floor
fridge
kitchen
Lester
oh!
played
swept
washed
your

Unit 13
arm
can't
cook
cooked
cut up
dinner
every
fell
garden
hard
hurt
over
Paul
picked
picking
pot
vegetables
worked

Unit 14
bring
children
Children's Day
China
curry
everyone
fun
India
Jamaica
let's
Miss Brown
noodles
picnic
rice
saltfish
share
tomorrow
yes

Unit 15
August
before
Big Parade
bird
blue mahoe tree
but
celebrations
cleaned
contest
days
Doctor Bird
drama
festival
festivals
flag
flower
fruit
important
Independence Day
join
Labour Day
last
lignum vitae
national
May
our
parade
parents
queen
runners-up
song
speech
symbols
there
watch
windows
winners
yard

Unit 16
afternoon
bag
band
box
cheered
clowns
Doctor Birds
dress up
excited
feathers
green
hurray!
opened
red
saw
yellow

Unit 17
bedroom
daddy
goes
Kevin
living room
moving
new
people
sofa
stove
truck
welcome

Unit 18
cooks
makes
pans
pots
sink
sit
soup
table

Unit 19
Aunt May
broken
build

built
carpenter
cleaner
down
frame
good
helped
Kayleigh
Lewis
night
roof
Sam
tiler
tiles
wind
windy
wooden

Unit 20
cooking
dropped
going
I'm
lid
near
never
picked up
ran
silly
sorry
yams

Unit 21
bathroom
books
canteen

car park
cars
games
Grade One
library
lunch
office
park
play
playground
playing field
principal
principal's
read
staffroom
teachers
wash

Unit 22
bell
best
both
dancing
end
Language Arts
Mr Wilson
music
playtime
rang
reading
Sandy
singing
writing

Unit 23
broke

chair
Dan
desk
did
dinosaur
door
goodbye
heavy
home
long
oh dear!
painted
paintbrush
pencil
tail
window
wrote

Unit 24
bad
better
bins
garbage
it's
Jasmine
Mary
mop up
mud
path
pull up
that
them
weeds

Unit 25
about

fire
fire bell
fire drill
fireman
just
Mr Jackson
rang
rings
talked
walked
well done

Unit 26
bumped
fast
fell over
listen
Miss Williams
Mr Nelson
rules
stairs

Unit 27
cleaners
Miss Jones
Miss Smith
Mr Harris
Mr Luke
Mr Winston
Mrs Bell
Mrs Porter
Mrs Taylor
janitor
secretary
these

vice-principal
watchman

Unit 28
Andrew
hospital
leg
nurse
tells
uniform
wear
why

Unit 29
ball
claps
cup
Jade
jumping
net
race
Red House
running
Sports Day
throw
throwing
time
tired
today
way
winner
wins

Unit 30
ate
balloons
Bevon
blew up
Cassey
got
ice cream
Miss Sharpe
party